Guide to the Mindful Awareness Perspective

How Mindfulness Works

Frank WJ Anderson MD MPH

Copyright

Copyright © 2025 by Frank William Joseph Anderson MD published by Camistin Publishing.

All rights reserved.

No portion of this book may be reproduced in any form without written permission from the publisher except as permitted by U.S. copyright law. Requests to the publisher for permission should be made to Camistin Publishing, Las Vegas, Nevada.

Guide to the Mindful Awareness Perspective: How Mindfulness Works

E-book ISBN 978-1-62408-024-1

Trade Paperback ISBN 978-1-62408-025-8

Hard Cover ISBN 978-1-62408-026-5

Camistin Publishing books are available wherever books are sold.

This publication is intended to provide accurate and helpful information on the subject matter covered. It is distributed with the understanding that neither the author nor the publisher is engaged in rendering legal, investment, medical, psychological, or other professional services. The content is for educational and informational purposes only and does not establish a physician-patient relationship. If you require medical, psychological, or other professional advice or services, please consult a qualified provider in your area. While the author and publisher have made every effort to ensure the accuracy and completeness of the information in this book, they make no representations or warranties, express or implied, regarding its content. They specifically disclaim any implied warranties of merchantability or fitness for a particular purpose and shall not be liable for any damages arising from its use.

Mindful Awareness Perspective™ is a trademark of the Mindful Awareness Institute, LLC, awaiting final registration. While the phrase may be used descriptively throughout the book, formal use of the Mindful Awareness Perspective as a training program or professional offering, is protected and may not be used without written permission. Readers and teachers are welcome to incorporate the phrases, metaphors and language in their own personal practice and teaching, with attribution appreciated. For licensing, collaboration, or training inquiries, please visit .

First edition 2025

Dedication

For Lisa Barry, who walked into the room quietly, asked the real questions, and never stopped exploring. Your voice, your courage, and your willingness to go deep on the air and in life helped this work take form. Though we never named it then, you lived the Mindful Awareness Perspective with grace, grit, and honesty. This book would not exist without you. Thank you for showing up. Thank you for staying open. You made it home.

And now, many others can too.

Acknowledgments

With gratitude to the many teachers and teachings that have helped shape the understandings and truths reflected here. David Knight, the Thai monks at Suan Mokkh, the Korean Buddhists, Adyashanti, Lisa Barry, Tara Brach, Jack Kornfield, Rupert Spira, Alan Watts, Eckhart Tolle, Byron Katie, Ram Dass, Marc Lesser and the many unnamed others who shared something essential. And to the ones who taught them—back through the generations to those who were brave enough to turn away from the status quo, to seek, and then to share.

This offering is part of that ongoing stream.

Prologue

The Mindful Awareness Perspective didn't arrive fully formed. It emerged slowly, subtly from the conversations, questions, challenges, and discoveries that unfolded over many months as Lisa Barry and I created the Exploring Awareness podcast. The core ideas were always present, but it was through the living interaction with Lisa as my co-host that they took shape. Lisa was not just a journalist asking questions, she was doing the work. She questioned everything, pushed back, saw her own barriers, and kept going. She worked harder than anyone I've known to move through confusion and resistance, in public for everyone to see. She eventually came to embody what I am now calling the Mindful Awareness Perspective. Interestingly, we never used those three words together in any of our episodes. They came to me later, as I contemplated the conversations we had over the 62 episodes of the podcast. The way this material is presented now, in a low-barrier, easily-accessible way is as much a reflection of Lisa's journey as it is of mine. This book is a continuation of the exploring awareness work we began together.

I met Lisa Barry one Thursday evening at the center where I taught mindfulness classes. She arrived quietly, slipping into the back of the room. I remember noticing her presence, not intrusive, not fully participating—more of an observer than a seeker. At the time, I had no idea who she was.

As the weeks went by and she began attending other sessions with different teachers, I came to learn that she was a journalist and reporter for one of our local NPR stations in Ann Arbor, WEMU. She had come to this role after a very different career—years spent on commercial radio, co-hosting a Detroit morning show filled with banter, festival broadcasts, and the kind of surface-level entertainment that left her seeking something more.

She made the courageous move from commercial radio to public radio, a shift that wasn't just about the work, but about finding deeper meaning and connection in her life. WEMU was a community-focused station full of passion projects incorporating jazz, eclectic music, and local voices. And that was where Lisa found her true voice.

One of her personal projects at WEMU was a weekly program called Art and Soul, where she poured her heart into exploring topics that mattered—art, food, music, social movements, and, occasionally, the spiritual path.

That's how our paths formally crossed. She invited me for an interview on Art and Soul to talk about mindfulness and my approach to mindful awareness.

We recorded the interview, and after the microphones were off, something shifted. Lisa's professional curiosity turned personal. She had so many questions—earnest, searching questions. I could hear the struggle in her voice, trying to figure it all out, reaching for understanding, and feeling the confusion that so often comes when the mind is wrestling with concepts the heart already knows.

At a certain point, I suggested that instead of talking about it, we just stop and meditate.

She was flustered by that. Here? Now? Where?

I suggested we head to the conference room. And there, in that ordinary space, I guided her through a meditation based on the Four Foundations of Mindfulness.

When it was over, she was visibly moved, excited, and alive in a way that wasn't intellectual but deeply felt. She asked me to do it again, to record it, and add it to the interview website so others could experience it too. So we did, and that recording is still available online today, the link here .

As I was gathering my things to leave, I turned to her casually and said, "You know… we should do a podcast." She laughed. A deep, knowing laugh. "Everyone says that" she told me, "but nobody ever follows through." But this time, I did.

And from that simple moment of shared stillness and openness, the Exploring Awareness podcast was born.

At the time, neither of us knew that we were stepping into something larger than ourselves. We didn't have language for it yet, but what we were really exploring was the very perspective derived from exploring awareness that would later become the foundation for the Mindful Awareness Perspective—MAP.

It was there, already present, quietly shaping our conversations and experiences. The awareness we spoke about wasn't theoretical; it was alive, making itself known through each breath, each pause, and each unexpected turn in the conversation.

In hindsight, that first interview wasn't just a broadcast but a beginning. The first footstep on a path we didn't yet know we were walking. And that's the beauty of awareness: it's always here, waiting patiently for us to notice. Even before we have the words, it's already leading the way.

Over time, we recorded 62 episodes together, each one a continuation of that first moment of discovery. In those episodes, Lisa's transformation became increasingly visible. At first, she, like many, tried to figure everything out. After a while, things shifted, and she wasn't just asking questions anymore; she was living the inquiry. In the process, she shed so much of what no longer served her and the old stories seemed to fall off. Something in her made a pivot, and she started to find her way home to the essential, the timeless. When you listen to the episodes in order from one to 62, her questions will resonate and you will witness and perhaps even share her transformation.

She came to call this process a Big Fun Journey and came to understand our podcast tagline—"Find Peace and Joy in the Most Unlikely Places"—in a deep and true way. Becoming aware of being aware—of everything good and bad—brought her to the joy of being and an embodiment of unconditional love. She found her Mindful Awareness Perspective and realized her authentic and original true self.

And then, unexpectedly, she passed away.

Episode 62 was fittingly titled "Return." Without knowing it, we had brought the arc of our shared exploration to a natural close. Episode 63 was mine alone—a moment of raw grief and open-hearted remembrance. I sat with that grief, reading David Whyte's poem *The Well of Grief*, and speaking directly from the awareness of that loss.

I was heartbroken. And yet, even in my heartbreak, there was a deep peace. A knowing. Not happy but realizing the "joy that has no opposite" from the awareness of the reality of the situation without resistance—immersed into the reality of what is. It was painful and joyful at the same time.

Lisa had returned.

She had touched and lived from the very essence we spoke about so often—the essence we all share—that unchanging awareness beneath the surface of our conditioned lives.

This is what the mystics mean when they say, *if you die before you die, you will not die when you die.*

Lisa had, in a very real sense, already died to part of her old self that wasn't serving her authentic self before she physically died. She shed the false self, the layers of conditioning and grasping, and returned home to her essential being. And so, even in her passing, I know she didn't truly die.

She lives on, not only in the recordings and the memories, but in the field of awareness itself—in that timeless bond we all share beyond the separation of time, form and identity. Her journey was a living testament to what is possible. It is a journey we can witness and traverse in our own way. And now, having distilled out from our work the Mindful Awareness Perspective, the work continues—not as something new to strive for, but as a reminder of what has always been here, waiting quietly for us to return.

Contents

1. Introduction — 1
2. Opening the MAP — 6
3. That's Great—But How? — 11
4. Your Compass Points the Way — 15
5. The Landscape — 17
6. Welcome to HACKlandia — 20
7. The 4+2 Path—The Map to the MAP — 28
8. Awareness of Breath — 32
9. Awareness of Body — 35
10. Awareness of Thoughts — 41
11. Awareness of Emotions — 46
12. Awareness of Awareness — 49
13. The Unity of All Beings — 53
14. Discovering and Living from a New Kind of Knowing — 56
15. Beyond This Way and That Way Is a Third Way — 60
16. Beyond Detachment—The MAP of Authentic Engagement — 63

17. Living from MAPtopia	66
18. Simple Daily Practices	69
Epilogue: The Path Continues	72
About the Author	74
Appendix I: Where to Go From Here	77
Appendix II: A Journey of Exploring Awareness	88

Chapter One

Introduction

How mindfulness works becomes clear when you discover what within you chaos has never touched. Timeless, stable, it transcends all the noise and chaos of the world we live in. When we arrive, we find that the defining elements of being human aren't shaped by outside influences but by our own innate nature—one that is shared by every person.

Your intention to start this journey is your compass. The trail is clearly marked, with stops along the way. The journey will be easy for some, difficult for others, but it is a well-worn path undertaken in one way or another by people over the ages. At first it may be very relaxing, and there are beautiful things to see. As you go along boulders will need moving, trails will need clearing, and steep sections will test you. It will take patience, and you will probably have to start over many times. When you reach the destination, you will find it is unlike any other—not an end but a beginning, the start of a new path that is defined only by the treasure you find. The journey and the destination become the same thing. It is then you live a life that is yours. It is the start of a new journey traversing your world with fresh eyes, shorn of what was obscuring them in the first place.

This book is your guide for that journey. This book is different. It's not about collecting more information or figuring something out. This book starts with a presumption: a source of wisdom and clarity that already exists within you. The constant demands of life and your ingrained habits cover it up. When you begin to see your life with mindful awareness, that inner knowing reveals itself. This is how mindfulness works. This inner knowing is the treasure.

Since this isn't something you can figure out with the usual ways of knowing, you might feel uncertain or think this isn't for you. That's a natural response. But if you're willing to read this book with openness, it will allow you to access what you already have but may not fully recognize.

Familiar ways of knowing can prevent the discovery of deeper treasure.

If you come to this book with expectations for a quick fix, they may not be met. You'll likely notice your inner critic becoming active as this book challenges your assumptions at a deep level, and your mind will turn this into criticism that urges you to stop reading. If you read this book and discover what the Mindful Awareness Perspective is about, you'll get to watch that critic activate and, using a deeper inner resource, see whether the critic is right. You then have a chance to open to what else might be true. It is possible to transform these thoughts into presence, and this book will show you how. If this book brings up something uncomfortable, you can ask why, and in that inquiry, a new understanding may be revealed. You won't know unless you continue reading.

Words are the only way we can communicate in a book, but the words themselves are just pointers. Focusing too much on the words distracts from where the words are pointing. If you get caught up on the words, if you're always finding a counterpoint or an error, you'll miss the point. Read this book for what it is, not for what it is not or what your prior knowledge tells you it should. Words have their place, but here the words are not even important. Here the words point to something beyond words and explanation. This book is called a Guide to the Mindful Awareness Perspective because the words point to the place of awareness that is aware of words, not the words themselves, connecting you to a universal reality through mindful awareness.

If you feel drawn to accessing and returning to your inner dimension, your true nature, your essential self, approach this book as an invitation. Read it openly. Welcome the critic and the doubts when they arise, but don't let them have the final say.

When you open like this, you'll encounter other challenges beyond the intellectual ones. We all carry deeply held beliefs about the world, and while this book doesn't ask you to believe anything specific, it will bring up an examination of held beliefs. We hold onto beliefs because they provide structure and identity, and when that gets questioned, our natural response is defensiveness. Throughout history, and even today, people defended their fixed beliefs with great intensity, holding on tightly because threatening those beliefs feels like threatening the very sense of self. You may notice this happening within you—a part that wants to nope out, and step away from what feels uncertain.

But here's something to consider: what if, instead of needing blind faith, you could have direct knowing? When Carl Jung was asked if he believed in God, he looked at the interviewer with a puzzled expression. He didn't need to believe in God—he knew God directly. True knowing doesn't require beliefs, and when you know something this deeply, you don't have to wait for some future moment to experience it—it's already here, already present.

If you feel called toward a deeper knowing, this guide offers a clear path. You'll discover that whatever beliefs you currently hold that are good and aligned with your true nature will become deeper and richer, and beliefs that no longer serve you will naturally fall away.

I chose the words for this book carefully. You will not find statements that tell you what you should or need to do. For those authors who do use those terms, it doesn't come from a paternalistic or demanding stance, but rather from a compassionate place that seeks to push you towards your own realization. In the past, I was reactive to these kinds of statements, but now I see them as they were intended. For this book, though, I have tried my best to present this as an invitation, your choice. A choice you may make now, or later, or on and off.

Also notice the use of verbs. Nouns often suggest a destination, a final accomplishment. Verbs suggest an ongoing action, a never-ending process. Will you ever know who you are, really? Or is it in the knowing? The Now is not a noun. It is being present. The Now ends as soon as you name it. Being allows you to dwell in it. When you see the verbs, use them as a reminder that there is no final destination to reach—only the ongoing journey that becomes the destination itself.

The fear of losing parts of identity and ego that come with old beliefs may feel real, and that's natural—your ego wants to protect what feels safe and familiar. So be aware if fear and defensiveness pop up. Remember that as you deepen through this perspective, bringing loving awareness to all thoughts, reactions, and emotions, they will transform into presence. A deeper layer of knowing will emerge. An awareness of everything will transform how you see and exist in the world.

In this process, you lose nothing essential and gain everything meaningful. People who have released their grip on ego often radiate true character and authenticity.

If you're seeking a grounded, authentic way of being in the world, if you want to connect with an inner essence that guides you, read this entire book with awareness, patience and kindness toward yourself. When the mental chatter and reactions arise—and they will—simply notice them with curiosity. Watch them come and go like clouds in the sky, without getting distracted, judgmental, or overly critical.

The older you get, the more fixed you become with familiar thoughts and beliefs, which makes it feel harder to let them shift when they no longer serve you. It's like accumulating stuff in your house over the years—the more things gather and clutter, the more effort it takes to create space. Don't wait until later—now is the time to start exploring awareness. But whatever your age or stage in life, you can step into this exploration and you will discover a welcoming, supportive place to land, and a treasure that's been waiting for you all along.

I trust that if you stay with this book all the way through, what it points to will reveal itself, opening a new way of being that is truly yours.

Chapter Two

Opening the MAP

What I am offering here is a low-barrier, easy-access way to understand deeper truths, distilled from books, beliefs, retreats, podcasts, and from my experience with the people with whom I've worked. What I'm offering isn't meant to replace or criticize any religion or tradition. It's simply another way to see what so many wise teachers have always pointed to. A fresh way that asks nothing new or foreign from you. A way that doesn't require you to adopt a new culture or identity.

I have found that many of the methods of teaching mindfulness and meditation are wrapped in the conditioning and language of the cultures from which they emerged. Forest monks, Korean masters, American therapists, Soto Zen, and Catholic contemplation have all shaped my path. Each has its own beauty. But each also comes with a form, a language, a way of being that can be hard to enter if it's not your world. After many years of struggling with different types of meditation and exploring various spiritual communities, and after a career in academic medicine, global health, working on the Navajo Nation, teaching and working closely with students in the clinical world and in the community at large, I've come to understand something that is important to share.

What I am inviting you to explore comes before culture, before beliefs, before thoughts.

At some point, I began to see that all these traditions point to the same root. But instead of starting there, I've found that many people are being dropped in at the middle—into the cultures, phrases, conclusions, practices and techniques that are born from years of deep realization by the people who teach them. "Let go," "You are not the self," and "Thoughts are just thoughts." These are all beautiful truths—but when given as instructions, or seen as expectations, they can lead to a sense of confusion rather than clarity.

If you can't "let go", if you can't "stop your thoughts", then what? You're left feeling like you're doing it wrong and that's not the case.

The same goes for meditation. It's often presented as the core method for finding peace and joy—but for many, meditation feels like a hill too steep to climb. I hear assumptions all the time like "I can't meditate," "I have other ways to zone out," or "I can't stop my thoughts." These assumptions about meditation are misguided. Too often, people are taught the technique before they understand to what it's pointing. Orientation comes before instruction. In this book, we begin with that orientation—what meditation is pointing to—before we learn the techniques.

Many of us feel a hunger for truth, for meaning, for peace, but when trying to enter through the middle, through established systems, we may get lost or discouraged, further supporting our misguided assumptions.

I want to pull things all the way back to the beginning, to the root.

When you start there, then the way forward becomes your own. Maybe that means understanding the roots of your own religion or exploring other cultures or traditions. Maybe it means practicing in your own quiet way. Maybe what you are doing seems like spiritual entertainment without a base. Knowing your root, you're moving from a place of grounded insight, not expectation.

Just to be clear: this is not a critique of any teachers or their teachings. I have deep gratitude for all of them. They're doing what they were trained to do, offering what their cultures and curricula taught them, and sharing the deep insights, traditions and techniques born from their own deep realization. What I'm saying is that the option exists to pause and turn our attention, not to the tradition, but to the root of what the tradition is about.

From there, you might find this enhances a tradition you already practice, or you may discover a new tradition or teacher that resonates deeply—entering from a place of recognition and clarity.

What I'm sharing is not something I made up. Everything presented here is grounded in ancient insights thousands of years old. What's different here is the frame. I'm offering my interpretation as a way of exploring that I hope makes this more accessible with a low barrier for entry, especially for those who have felt blocked, confused, or alienated. And if you've never investigated material like this before, even better—you will be learning clearly from the root.

We've come to think of mindfulness as a tool for self-help or self-improvement, and in some cases for improved productivity or accepting the status quo. Sometimes referred to as McMindfulness. It can be presented as a treatment for stress, depression, and anxiety. But what I'm talking about here is not just for your stress reduction or your boss's bottom line. It's about how the peace, joy, love and compassion that you discover already in yourself is an essence inherent to your very being that can ripple outward and become a force in the world. This is a way forward, especially in times like these.

The information in this book offers a path to a simple, accessible, experiential perspective—the Mindful Awareness Perspective, or the MAP. Living a life from this perspective provides insights and bandwidth informed not by established habits and conditioning, but by realizing, at a deep level, the inherent qualities of being human.

This book provides a "map" to the MAP, guiding us all to our shared essence, naturally and authentically. We come to realize that everyone has this same innate nature which then allows us to move around in the world in a new way, informed by the knowledge we gain from these realizations, and by putting them into action.

The map to the MAP begins not by technique, but by a shift or pivot to an awareness stance—a place where a stable and open sense of being aware emerges as a conscious layer of everyday life. A layer that's been there all along, but not realized, not consciously seen.

Connecting to your mindful awareness perspective does not ask you to give up thoughts and reason, or to become an emotionless zombie. It doesn't require that you meditate, suppress your thoughts, act a certain way, be a vegetarian, or any other preconceived notions you may have about mindfulness and meditation. It simply is a return to your natural and authentic self.

So let's not start with the technique, let's start with what's behind it. If we look at the realization first, then doing the practices that support that realization can emerge naturally. The techniques won't be something extra on your to-do list, but something you want to do—not out of striving, but because they feel like home. This is how we let our inner life evolve without loading it up with new expectations or goals. We bring everything into awareness. And yes, at first that might feel like mental awareness—and that's fine. But soon, awareness of your conditioning can open into something deeper: ***awareness of awareness itself***.

In that silent space, a deeper realization begins to emerge—a connection to essence, a sense of unity, a quiet knowing, and a natural connection to all things.

I believe you've already glimpsed this. Most people have, at least once. And you can live from that place, too. Rather than chasing after it, you shift your perspective. That's what the Mindful Awareness Perspective (MAP) is here for. It's not the final thing to learn, but a way to reveal what's behind it all.

And when that becomes clear, what to do next becomes obvious.

Chapter Three

That's Great—But How?

The question is—how do we come to the place where we realize our true nature, our inherent selves? We open this door to a mindful awareness perspective by first setting an intention and developing an interest in being aware of what is going on in the present moment. This is the compass, pointing us to the awareness layer that sees the entirety of the body and its functions as an object of awareness, eventually as a whole but starting with sections. We can focus on certain activities of the body—like awareness of the breath, body, thoughts, or emotions. With a mindful awareness perspective, you see everything the mind and body are doing together from this field of awareness. And when you have a steady MAP, and the awareness of this awareness, something interesting happens— you now expand your identity and rest outside of habits, thoughts, conditions, judgments, and fixed knowledge. You are just fully present and experiencing a sense of peace and joy and love that is innate and authentic.

This book is not meant to teach you how to meditate. We will use some techniques derived from Buddhist traditions and modern mindfulness techniques along the way. These techniques support your discovery and continuation of a mindful awareness perspective. You don't have to meditate, but you may find yourself spending more and more time with these techniques as you begin to realize that they support the MAP and the groundedness it brings. I will describe these techniques and how to use them in later chapters, but the implied obligation and necessity of this vague term meditation prevent many people from discovering their deeper selves.

I'll be using a few metaphors throughout this book to help communicate the ideas more easily. The first is based on the acronym HACK, for Habits, Assumptions, Conditioning, and (fixed)Knowledge—we'll call the place where our actions, decisions, judgments, and motivations arise from, HACKlandia. The second part of the metaphor describes the place we occupy when we experience life through the Mindful Awareness Perspective—we'll call that MAPtopia. In this metaphorical story, we go on a journey of exploring awareness, starting in HACKlandia as we know it today, and following a path with four stops and two realizations—the 4+2 Path—that leads us to MAPtopia. From there, we return to HACKlandia, but we are no longer the same. We carry with us the innate knowledge and wisdom we've uncovered, not the rigid certainty of fixed knowledge and we begin to live a life informed and aligned by the essences we now embody as a result of this journey.

The invitation to go on this journey provides an opportunity to expand how life is lived and experienced. The journey will take us through a variety of landscapes along the way—there are beautiful expansive vistas to enjoy and hard mountains to climb. There are sunrises and sunsets, there are fields and swamps. It is a round trip where you begin to realize innate knowledge and perspectives that were just waiting to emerge. When you return from the journey, you will find things different than when you started. The things you thought you knew weren't as important, or heavy, or so urgent anymore. Realizations emerge during the journey that you never paid attention to before, and you are surprised no one ever taught you this. This new knowledge and perspective does not result in gaining new factual knowledge. Rather, as you see the hacks, they begin to drop away, and something new begins to emerge—new information, a deeper kind of knowing, the knowingness you can't learn from facts alone.

Contrary to popular belief, this is not about stopping thoughts. It's about pivoting attention. From your phone, from your worry, from the past and future—from the path you were unconsciously on. Just pivot to a mindful awareness perspective. That's the move. The simplest action in sports, in dance, in life: pivot. When you do, you'll notice something. There is a shift. You become the one who's aware. You're no longer just the one thinking—you're the one noticing the thinking. And right there, you've broken the spell. You are living guided by the awareness realized through a mindful awareness perspective.

But here's the hard part: most people's minds will talk them out of this pivot before they even start. Or if they do start, their minds will convince them it's not working or not worth continuing. Why? Because this perspective threatens the habitual mind. It undercuts the entire structure of identity that people have unconsciously used to build their sense of self. I'm pointing to a moment. One moment. Right now. This is about stopping, pivoting, and noticing what's always been: your own innate awareness. I invite you to start the journey of exploring awareness. Pivot to a mindful awareness perspective. Be aware. Be aware of being aware. And see what opens up. It's already here. You don't have to earn it. You don't have to let go. Just stop. Pivot. Things fall off. And you will see what emerges.

Chapter Four

Your Compass Points the Way

This entry point is simple, and your internal compass points the way. The compass orients you to bring awareness to the things that are already happening—your breath, your body, your thoughts, your emotions. It's always pointing towards MAPtopia, you just take out the compass, look at it and follow the arrow. Use the map to the MAP anytime, anywhere.

Your breath and body are doing their thing, most of the time without you noticing. The same is true of your thoughts and emotions. They just keep rolling. When you can bring awareness to the breath and body, you can bring it to your thoughts and emotions too. It's the same move. It's like shining a light on what's been running in the background. And this first move—this pivot—is only the beginning. Because when you begin to know yourself as awareness, not just as someone trying to be aware, another door opens. And through that door is a whole different world. A world of insight. A world of wisdom. A world of wonder. A realization of the essences of unconditional love, the joy of being, the peace that surpasses understanding, and the solid ground of compassion for yourself and others. Seeing your compass, following the 4+2 Path to the Mindful Awareness Perspective in MAPtopia, you can look so deeply into your inner world that it's almost startling. You begin to see how your mind works, how you formed your patterns, how emotions layered themselves, and how you built reactions on top of memories and defenses. You can dissect what's going on inside with incredible clarity.

It can be scary territory. It's not for the faint of heart. It's for the curious, the brave, the ones willing to look and follow their internal compass. And what you'll find there will be amazing, frightening, painful, surprising, and inspiring all at once. You might see how you've wrapped pain in pleasure. How your view of the world was shaped when you were a child—and how you've been carrying that version of reality forward, tying yourself up without even knowing it. But once you realize a mindful awareness perspective, all of these things become transformed into present moment awareness. Things start to shift; the tight knots begin to loosen. And you're not just someone mired in problems anymore, you are what is present to whatever is. HACKlandia dissolves into presence with a mindful awareness perspective: you're now seeing and feeling clearly from a stable, strong, compassionate knowing.

Chapter Five

The Landscape

Each of us begins life as a single cell—the result of billions of years of incredible events in the universe. We arrived on a planet that uniquely suits complex biochemical processes, culminating in a one-of-a-kind combination of atoms that program and orchestrate our biological existence.

The events that created this universe: the particular configuration of our solar system, the protection from meteors Earth receives from Jupiter's gravity, Earth's own composition, and countless other synchronicities are prerequisites for our being here. Our own unique DNA is the outcome of millions of years of evolutionary pressure and the successful reproduction of our ancestors all the way back to single-celled organisms. Survival of the fittest, the friendliest, the cleverest, the most aggressive all contributed to what we are today.

Starting as a single-celled potential, we completed a quiet gestational period, simply existing in the darkness of the womb. Then, it was disrupted. We entered the air-based world of light, sound, and changing temperature, and others proclaimed us male or female and gave us a name. We took our first breath—and have continued to do so ever since.

Your parents and guardians who have their own histories received you and who, in the only way they knew how, provided you with food, protection, and care. You survived. You survived the many biological forces that might have ended your life, unlike so many others in this world.

The place you were born, the color of your skin, your assigned biological sex—all began to shape how others saw you, and how you began to see yourself. Society and culture had already extensively conditioned the people you were born to. That conditioning was important to them, and they treated you accordingly. You absorbed it because you knew no other way. Your rapidly developing brain aligned with your caregivers. Personality and identity emerged as you mimicked those around you. This was unconscious. In a sense, you had no choice. You had to do this to be accepted and cared for.

You learned what to say, how to behave, what to believe. They told you what was right and wrong, who you could trust and who you couldn't. Your caregivers shaped your preferences. They disciplined you when you went astray. Your caregivers might have been joyful or angry, peaceful or volatile—but their behavior, their words, and their reactions shaped how you moved through the world. You entered school. You learned rules of behavior, interaction, and performance. You faced successes and failures.

Then, through the upheaval of adolescence, reproductive hormones changed your biology. A deep urge to reproduce began to influence your decisions and motivations, shaped by the social world around you. Eventually, like all animals, you had to become an independent adult—armed with your conditioning, your habits, your assumptions, and whatever knowledge you'd acquired. You moved into the world to conquer it or be conquered by it.

So here we are.

Each of us is the result of those biological and social realities. Yes, it's complicated. But in simple terms, we are a product of our habits, our assumptions, our conditioning, and our knowledge. Hacked to live successfully in the world we were born into. Like it or not, believe it or not, this is, in our own mind—either entirely or to a large extent—who we are today.

Or is it?

Chapter Six

Welcome to HACKlandia

A hack can be defined as a clever tip or technique for doing or improving something, or a quick and often effective solution to a problem perhaps with a bit of "creative improvisation." In this metaphor, the word hack refers to the part of our lives that has been an ingenious, if makeshift, solution to staying alive and being in a world defined by others and our assumptions about it. In simple terms, we live in HACKlandia—a landscape formed by the amalgamation of biological necessity, social programming and the habits and assumptions that come with it. Not bad, not good; just the way it is.

HACKlandia is where most of us live, most of the time. It's familiar. It's predictable. It's comforting in a way, even if it's also confining. We are "HACKed," and all the inputs we've received shaped and sculpted us since before we were even born. Some good ones of course, and some that aren't of service now. Sometimes we feel like we wake up, plug into our roles, follow our routines, and rarely question why we do what we do. If we do question, and don't have an answer, we then suppress. Some days it feels like we are wind-up toys released in the morning, set to repeat yesterday with minor variations.

This is not to say HACKlandia is "bad." It's not. In many ways, it keeps society functioning. It teaches us how to survive, how to work, how to relate. We create amazing things and sometimes have a wonderful time. But it also limits us. Because HACKlandia is not who we are, it's where we've been living.

HACKlandia has many neighborhoods. Each one serves a function, and some are useful—necessary, even—for getting through daily life. But some of them keep us locked into identities, patterns, and perspectives that make it hard to see things clearly or experience the fullness of who we are.

Figuring-It-Out-Ville is where the mind never stops spinning. In this neighborhood, people try to analyze their way into clarity, forcing experiences into logical frameworks. It's the land of strategies, flowcharts, and self-help books. This is the default setting for those of us who believe that enough thinking will eventually solve everything—including our suffering. When we try to describe awareness—true, expansive, present-moment awareness—the residents here immediately start carving it up into categories, distinctions, conclusions. That's how they've been taught to know things: figure it out, label it, organize it.

Judgment Heights is a place perched high above the inner world. From here, we evaluate everything—our performance, our thoughts, our bodies, other people. Everything gets a rating. This place is run by the Inner Critic and the Comparison Police. Here, even our attempts at self-awareness get graded.

Down the road is Reaction Alley. Something happens—you get cut off in traffic, someone criticizes you—and boom, you're off. Instant reaction. No pause, no breath. Just the automatic firing of a neural pathway built decades ago. This is where the nervous system runs the show, driven by a thousand past experiences.

Identity Square is a vibrant neighborhood filled with masks, roles, and social scripts. You might be a parent, a doctor, a teacher, a partner—each role with its own expectations. These identities become so embedded that we forget they're just roles. We think they're us.

And there is a Museum in HACKlandia that you can visit to see all of your past in great detail, all of the things you did right (which you sometimes overlook) and all the things you did wrong (which you stare at for hours). Reliving the past is your biological hack trying to keep you safe, from repeating the same mistakes twice, to figure out what you should or should not have done. Here, you revisit the pain, the disrespect, the unmet assumptions and those false needs that were never met. You look at the dioramas and think it should have been different, it's not right. These exhibits build up over time, taking up more and more space, reinforcing negative attitudes.

The Theater is where your future gets revealed. The movies and plays shown here lay out with certainty what the future holds. It's dramatic and suspenseful, the way we are so certain that we know what is going to happen. It comes with dread or excitement but either way, we are absolutely sure that because we saw it on the stage, or on the news, or because everyone else thinks it is going to happen, it will. It's so realistic we live in the future as if it is happening right now. The bad predictions create great fear, fear of the known or the unknown—it draws us in and occupies our minds. We go home and lock our doors. This part of HACKlandia is so compelling and contagious. So much so that if you don't buy into the common view of the future, you will find yourself alone in HACKlandia.

And let's not forget Spiritual Bypassing Boulevard. This neighborhood looks different—lots of incense and affirmations and spiritual entertainment—but it's still HACKlandia. It's where we use spiritual language or practices to avoid the discomfort of actually facing ourselves. It's a softer kind of avoidance, but avoidance all the same.

HACKlandia rests on a kind of fixed knowledge that is useful but incomplete. It's the kind of knowledge you can look up, write down, teach, test. As a doctor, I've spent a lifetime acquiring this kind of knowledge. It saves lives. But I've also come to see that it doesn't tell the whole story of what it means to be human. In HACKlandia, we tend to confuse knowledge with wisdom. We think that knowing more facts will make us more whole. We try to fix our emotional pain with intellectual solutions. We analyze our way out of grief. We strategize our way into love. We try to think our way to peace.

The knowledge here is fixed, rigid and certain. It is as if the knowledge we have is complete. To question is an offense, leading to arguments about who is right, where "right" is what is in my fixed knowledge base. To say "I don't know" is anathema to many people and may be seen as a sign of weakness. But remember, the knowledge in HACKlandia derives from the particular habits, conditions, and assumptions that we have absorbed along the way. It is limited, it is incomplete and much of it may not even be true. This part of HACKlandia is very difficult to see without a mindful awareness perspective. HACKlandia keeps us locked in our heads. It's top-down.

And here's the tricky part: we don't even realize we're in HACKlandia. We think we're just living our lives. We assume that our thoughts are us. That our moods are reality. That our reactions are justified. We don't see the programming—we only feel the output. It is like being an AI system that can only output variations of what others input and we processed. While this autopilot mode serves certain functions, it also limits us from accessing our fuller potential.

But now the question arises: is this all there is? Inputs and outputs? Social success or failure? Repetition of patterns we didn't choose? Is it satisfying? Or is there something more? Maybe you've already unconsciously decided that this is all there is, and trying for something more is pointless. Maybe you've felt the deep sense that there is more, but don't know how to access it. That longing, unfulfilled, may have become the root of your anxiety, your depression, or your drive. Or maybe you believe in something because of a religion or philosophy you were taught—that if you do the right things, you'll gain access to something beyond this life.

But all of that—all of those reactions, beliefs, and structures—still belong to HACKlandia.

Now, perhaps for the first time, you're seeing it in totality.

There's something beyond all this. The past is gone, and the future is yet to come. Maybe all of the hacks in HACKlandia are obstructing our ability to see what is beyond. Every now and then, we catch a glimpse. A quiet moment. A sudden insight. A wave of peace. A spontaneous act of kindness. These moments come from somewhere else, somewhere more innate, beyond mere knowledge, from beyond HACKlandia.

It's a lot to take in. But remember how you began—as a pure being with biological conditioning, with a pure and absolute presence. As a practicing Obstetrician/Gynecologist, I see newborn babies all the time—they are pure, unconditioned, unhabituated present moment beings. Pure presence. That sense of presence is still in us today underneath all the layers of HACKlandia. You still have access to it. And sometimes, it breaks through in a spontaneous and fleeting way, like a bubble coming to the surface out of HACKlandia. It's time now to live full time on the surface.

The journey begins with exploring awareness. Exploring awareness starts with becoming aware that we live in a world of clever problem-solving—of hacks. And in that awareness, we can access our original identity as pure, present beings. When we were born, we were present. We didn't know it then—we just were. But now we have the opportunity to be aware of presence—we can be aware that we are aware. This is the beginning of the journey to the Mindful Awareness Perspective. But before we go there, we have to understand where we are. This is why we begin in HACKlandia. We begin by seeing it. Naming it. Getting to know its rules, its tricks, its comforts, and its limitations. Only by seeing it clearly can we begin to pivot to the MAP. Make no mistake—this pivot is not about escaping. It's not about rejecting everything you've ever learned. It's about seeing it from a new vantage point. It's about finding a path through HACKlandia, not around it. It's about being compassionate with the reality of our lives. It's about learning to walk the same streets with different eyes.

To explore the awareness of our lives in HACKlandia, start with bringing out your compass and the map to the MAP. The compass is your intention to live from a mindful awareness perspective. The map guides us along the 4+2 Path that leads through awareness points—breath, body, thoughts, and emotions, opens us to the awareness of awareness and the realization of the unity of all beings, and then gradually we return back to HACKlandia with a new sense of ourselves. As we cultivate and become aware of the MAP something remarkable happens. We open to a level of awareness that not only sees our thoughts, emotions, and conditioning, but recognizes: I am aware of these things. I am aware that I am aware and I realize that all beings, all things share the same

A deeper question emerges: What is aware of the fact that I have the MAP? And in that moment, in that space of pure presence beyond all thoughts, things become clear. HACKlandia dissolves. Not as something we destroy or escape, but as something seen for what it is—a clever structure that no longer runs the show. What's real, what remains, is the peace, joy, love and compassion—the essences that have always been right below the surface. And in that realization, you recognize that this is not only your essence—but the essence of every other human being. Every being. Everything.

MAPtopia is not a place. It's not a reward. It's not an ideal state you achieve by hard effort or merit. It is simply what is revealed when the filters of HACKlandia no longer obscure reality. It is what emerges when you no longer identify exclusively with your habits, assumptions, conditioning, and knowledge. In MAPtopia, you live from a mindful awareness perspective—still in this world, still human, still navigating life's terrain. But now, you see the terrain for what it is. You move with clarity, compassion, equanimity, and joy. And in doing so, you help others do the same—not by teaching them anything, but simply by being yourself.

As we move forward in our journey of exploring awareness, we'll discover this space where awareness becomes your guide instead of letting habit run the show. Where presence replaces programming. Where peace, joy, and compassion arise—not as goals, but as natural outcomes of seeing clearly.

You are invited to take this journey—to explore awareness, to awaken the perspective that's already within you, to rediscover what's never been lost.

That's the first step.

Awareness begins here.

Let's begin.

Chapter Seven

The 4+2 Path—The Map to the MAP

Exploring awareness with a map to the MAP takes us on the 4+2 Path. It starts simply with a compass—the intention to take a step out of HACKlandia for a minute or forty, have a look, and become aware of the context in which you live. Follow your internal compass. Taking a step out of HACKlandia is not an idea, a denial, a theory, or a belief. It is an intention to have a direct experience, right here, right now of anything and everything that is happening in the present moment. The map guides us along the 4+2 Path and gives us a systematic, easily remembered and repeatable way to do just that. And if you can't remember, just keep a physical copy of the map with you. Along the 4+2 Path, we will investigate six dimensions of the exploring awareness experience, each one offering a door into presence. The first four are your entry points—breath, body, thoughts, and emotions. These are the foundations. Each offers a unique perspective, while simultaneously being aspects of the same thing: the experience of being alive in this moment. The "plus two" are the deepening stages—awareness of awareness and the realization of the unity of all beings. They are not steps you earn or unlock. They arise naturally as you settle into presence and begin to see what has been here all along.

Let's take a look at them briefly (more complete descriptions are in the following chapters).

Awareness of Breath—The breath is your most immediate link to the present. You've been breathing your whole life, but have you been aware of it? Awareness of your breath is the first doorway to awareness. It's not about controlling the breath—it's about witnessing it. Letting it be. Letting yourself be. In the breath, we find rhythm, grounding, and a reminder that life continues moment by moment.

Awareness of Body—The body is not separate from the breath. When you inhale, the body expands; when you exhale, it softens. As you tune into the body, you start to feel its language—sensations, tensions, temperature shifts. These are messages from the present moment. Your body is your anchor. It's always here, even when your mind is racing.

Awareness of Thoughts—Thoughts arise like waves—predictable, repetitive, often reactive. By observing your thoughts, rather than getting swept away by them, you begin to see them for what they are: mental events. Not truths. Not commands. Just thoughts. This recognition creates space. Thoughts no longer trap you—now you recognize them—they simply arise and fall—like the breath—as aspects of your own being. You are witnessing thoughts from a layer of awareness.

Awareness of Emotions—Emotions are energy in motion, an expression of the thoughts' effects on the body. When you become aware of an emotion—without judgment, without analysis—you give it permission to move through you. Emotions arise and fall just like breath. Anger, sadness, joy, fear—they are visitors, not permanent residents. With awareness, you learn to greet them, feel them, and let them pass as they are transformed into presence.

Awareness of Awareness—This is the pivotal shift. Awareness of awareness means you're not just aware of the content—you're aware of the container. You become the witnessing, an active verb, the space in which everything arises. It's subtle. It's not a thought. It's an experience—a knowing (another verb) that you are not your thoughts, not your emotions, not your body or breath. You are the one who knows that you know. Awareness becomes a verb.

And it's from this vantage point—this resting as awareness—that something even more profound begins to emerge. Not because you went looking for it, but because it's what's already here, no longer obscured. From this stillness, the essences begin to reveal themselves. Not as concepts or feelings, but as qualities that arise naturally when the noise subsides. A Joy that has no opposite. A love that is unconditional. An inherent sens of equanimity and peace. Equanimity isn't indifference but presence. Compassion and loving-kindness flow without needing a reason. A wisdom that doesn't come from facts. Intuition that doesn't come from logic. Generosity that comes from fullness. Gratitude that arises simply because this is. These aren't things you strive to achieve. They emerge when the striving stops. They are recognized—not invented—as aspects of your own being. They come from the bottom up. And when these essences are experienced from awareness itself, something even deeper opens.

Unity of All Beings—As you rest in awareness and begin to sense these essences as your natural state, something profound emerges. A sense that you are not alone in this field of being. That this awareness is not yours or mine—it's shared. It's universal. The qualities you recognize in yourself—peace, love, joy, compassion—are not private possessions. They're reflections of something we all share. And in that, the illusion of separation begins to dissolve. You feel connected, not in a sentimental way, but in a deeply grounded way. This is not belief—it's direct experience.

Together, these six stops on the 4+2 Path form a complete, embodied path to presence. They are doors to walk through, again and again, in any order. They support each other. They interweave. They illuminate. And every time you return, you remember. You remember that you are not stuck in HACKlandia. You are already standing on the ground of awareness. Let the 4+2 Path be your journey to the MAP. Let it guide you home.

Chapter Eight

Awareness of Breath

As we start exploring awareness with the map to the MAP, we always start with the breath. Not just because it's simple, but because it's something we've been doing since our very first moment of life, an integral part of the present moment experience.

I have witnessed that miraculous first breath countless times. It's a moment that, now, never ceases to fill me with wonder. (Earlier in my career, I was too distracted to notice.) That first inhalation marks the beginning of life outside the womb—and it keeps going, breath after breath, moment after moment for the rest of that person's life.

You've been breathing your whole life, but have you ever really noticed your breath? You've been breathing for the last five minutes. Did you know that you were breathing? This unconscious breathing versus conscious awareness of breath is where our journey begins. The breath is our doorway into a mindful awareness perspective and the MAP. Not just a calming tool, not just a concentration object, it's the first and most natural anchor into presence. When we bring awareness to the breath, something changes. We're no longer just on autopilot. We become present. And presence is where everything begins. It doesn't mean we're trying to change the breath. You don't need to control the breath. It's perfect as it is. Our job is to notice it—to ride the waves of inhalation and exhalation to feel the subtle movements of the chest, ribs, and belly. Sometimes, it helps to feel it in specific places—like the nostrils or the rise and fall of the belly. Sometimes, just knowing you're breathing is enough. But in knowing that you are breathing, that shift from unconscious to conscious is what becoming aware is all about.

You'll get distracted. Of course you will. That's normal. We can expect that. But every time you notice that your mind has wandered, and you gently return to the breath, you are becoming aware. The breath becomes more than a physiological process. It becomes a teacher. A reminder that you are awareness. Awareness of breath is not the whole journey, but it's the front door. And it's always unlocked for you to open. Just look at your compass, use the MAP and find your way.

Although we often describe mindful awareness of the breath and body as separate steps on the 4+2 Path, the reality is that they're deeply interconnected. As you become more mindfully aware of your breath, you'll naturally begin to notice how it moves through your body, how it stretches you from the inside out. This awareness is not just of the physical aspects of breathing, but there are some cool physiological things happening to be aware of as well. As a physician, I've studied the intricate mechanics of respiration down to the cellular level, and while I won't take us down a rabbit hole of physiological detail here, I'll give you a glimpse of what's happening. When you take a breath in, you're drawing in air that's 21% oxygen, produced by plants, a lot of it coming from the ocean. That oxygen in the air enters the lungs and crosses an ultra-thin membrane and attaches to red blood cells. Those cells then travel through the heart and are pumped out to nourish every part of your body. Each cell, like a tiny engine, uses that oxygen to do its work—whether that's enabling thought, movement, or organ function. As with any engine, there's a byproduct (carbon dioxide). Your blood carries this waste product back to the lungs, where you release it with each exhalation. If the carbon dioxide builds up too much, it makes your blood acidic—a signal to your body to increase your rate of breathing. This is why you breathe faster when you're exercising. It's not just exertion—it's chemistry.

So, this breath that seems so simple is actually the driver of a beautifully choreographed dance. When you become aware of it, you're not just noticing air in and air out—you're tuning into a vast, living system of amazing hacks working to keep you alive. This is the magic of the breath as the first stop on the map to the MAP. It's always happening, always accessible, always available as a gateway to presence. And when you pay attention, even briefly, you're grounding yourself in reality—in something profoundly real, essential, and unchanging. You are realizing yourself as awareness, and becoming aware that you are aware.

This is the breath—not just as biology, but as your anchor to the present moment and an expression of the Mindful Awareness Perspective.

Take a few moments now to explore the awareness of the breath.

Chapter Nine

Awareness of Body

Let's talk about the body—not as an object or an afterthought, but as a living, breathing present moment experience. Many of us tend to ignore the body until it breaks down. We live in our heads, in screens, in thoughts. But the body is here, always present. And when we bring awareness of it, something shifts. The body scan is the next stop on the 4+2 Path, experiencing the body from a mindful awareness perspective. It happens by bringing attention, systematically, from head to toe (or vice versa), noticing the different parts of the body. I usually start with my feet and become aware of how my feet feel. (My feet don't like shoes, so they feel really good when I am out of my shoes and there's no weight on them). When you spend some time being aware of the feet, you will realize and be surprised how important the big toe is to balance. Then, like a handheld scanner, bring awareness up the legs, to the pelvis and abdomen and chest, then up the back, noticing all the muscles and organs and bones that exist there. Move the scanner up to the shoulders and let them relax, let all the muscles relax. Awareness lets you see that the muscles are tight, and with that seeing your muscles relax to their natural relaxed state. Did you notice that? You may not have been aware that you were carrying this muscle tension, and with awareness, it loosens. Now scan your hands, stopping to marvel at these amazing instruments of dexterity and sensation. Then move up the arms to the shoulders and neck and let awareness allow them to fall back to their normal state.

So now, you are becoming aware from your neck down of your entire body. You are out of your head. But as you will see, it's not your head that is providing the awareness. Now become aware of the head, the hair on your head, and all those facial muscles that you use to convey emotions. Become aware of facial muscles and they too relax, sometimes twitching before they finally get back to a baseline state. Explore the awareness of the senses, sight, hearing, smell, taste. Being aware of the senses is a big shift to a mindful awareness perspective. Now, let's become aware of what is inside the head. Your processing center. Become aware of your brain as an organ, like your lungs. Most of it is running unconsciously, keeping everything going. Maybe there is a vague awareness of the hum of those activities. The other parts of the brain are generating all the thoughts necessary for life in HACKlandia. It's holding past memories and future thinking that are linked to emotions. We will get to awareness of thoughts and emotions in the next two chapters, but for now, be aware of the brain as an organ doing what it does and applying a mindful awareness perspective to its function just like the breath. As you do this, are you becoming aware that you are aware that there is a layer of yourself emerging that is beyond the body and the brain? Stop here for a minute and feel into that. Be aware of how the body is now —without thinking about it. You might notice warmth, coolness, pressure, tingling. You might notice aliveness, you might notice... nothing. And that's fine too. As we bring awareness to the whole body as it is, we begin to feel the body as a whole—not just parts, not just aches and pains, but as a total field. Breath flows through it. Energy moves within it, and we are aware, and aware of that awareness.

Here's something interesting: your body is more than a thing you have. It's a very dynamic process that's always changing. Right now, your blood is flowing. Your nerves are firing. Your cells are doing their intricate dance with the oxygen and carbon dioxide processing. And all of it is happening in awareness. From a medical standpoint, I could describe this in great detail: the various organ systems, the muscles, bones, nerves, and arteries, all responding to the environment and body chemistry. But beyond the biology, there's an invitation: can you feel this? The weight of your body on the chair, the feeling of your feet on the floor?

Your body is your anchor to the present moment. You can't live in tomorrow or yesterday in your body. It's always perfectly present.

So, we begin to relate to the body differently—not as a vehicle to push, not as a source of shame or pride, but as a way to experience the present moment. As something sacred. And when you do this regularly you begin to realize not just the body, but the knowing of the body. The field in which all sensation arises. That's where the mindful awareness perspective leads—not to some special state, but to the one you're already in.

Before we go deeper down the 4+2 Path, allow me to go down the rabbit hole a bit to explore that humming quietly happening in the background: your nervous system. It's worth sharing how the MAP aligns with what we know about the body and brain. Because, when you understand this, the realizations become even more grounded—and even more amazing.

Your nervous system is always on. Always working. Always coordinating. It's responsible for how you stand upright, how you balance, how you feel pain, how you respond to a joke, or how you feel when someone frowns at you. It's not just sending signals. It's shaping your entire experience of being alive. Most of this is happening without your conscious input. The nervous system operates so efficiently, so automatically, that it becomes invisible. But when we bring awareness to the breath, to the body, to emotions and thoughts, what we're actually doing to a large degree, is bringing awareness to how the nervous system is functioning. This is not about controlling or fixing anything—it's about noticing. Watching. Observing with curiosity and compassion.

I remember during my medical training, learning the fine details of neurology, memorizing cranial nerves, studying complex pathways, learning the signs and symptoms of different neurological problems—it was both awe-inspiring and humbling. We are literally wired in our entire bodies with nerves. These allow us to sit upright, move, play, think, see, taste, smell, touch—all the senses are realized with a functioning nervous system. And next to those nerves are arteries and veins, carrying oxygen-rich blood to feed them. Glucose and oxygen, the fuel. Carbon dioxide, the exhaust. It's a constant metabolic exchange. When you become aware of that flow—when you feel the rhythm of the body, the pulsing aliveness—you're tuning into the biological machinery. But more than that, you're remembering that you are not that machinery. You're the one who knows it's running. Any glitch or damage or lack of oxygen can bring all or part of the system down. The nervous system is a masterpiece.

But what those lectures didn't touch on is what happens when we become aware of that system in action. No textbook captures the quiet miracle of what happens when someone becomes aware of their own awareness. In that moment, something shifts. The nervous system is still working—but we are no longer inside of it, entangled in its loops. We are witnessing it. We become aware of the processor, not just the programs. Imagine you're sitting in a data center. There's a computer in front of you—whirring, calculating, running code. Most people spend their lives as that computer, reacting and computing and responding. But with a mindful awareness perspective, we become the one observing in the room. The one who is seeing the machine working. Once you see it—you can't unsee it. You become aware of how your body adjusts itself in space. How your breath responds to emotion. How your thoughts spiral or settle. How your emotions rise like weather fronts and pass just the same.

It's like layering out. There are many levels to the human experience—and they're all happening at once. The norm is to walk around thinking there's only one layer, and that's the one coming through the nervous system. That makes sense. Our bodies are wired to perceive and process through that system. It's how we move, how we balance, how we survive. Try this: become aware of the nervous system that's holding your body upright right now. Feel the muscles, the subtle adjustments in posture, the tension or ease. In doing so, you've just accessed a new layer of experience—something beyond the system itself. You're no longer just a nervous system reacting. You're the awareness of it. This is what I mean by layered awareness. At first, it's physical: breath, blood, nerves, digestion. Then, it's psychological: thoughts, emotions, reactions. And then, it becomes something else—an awareness of awareness itself. A stillness that doesn't belong to the nervous system. A knowing that exists before, during, and beyond the activity of the body and mind.

And that's where the shift happens.

When we rest in this layer of knowing—this deeper awareness—we find a space untouched by our programming, our habits, or our histories. A space that has always been there. When we begin to live from that space, the whole story of the self begins to look different. Not discarded, not rejected—just held in a wider field. A truer context.

That's what this practice is about. And that's why we keep returning to the MAP: to orient ourselves in that vast field, and to live from it—layer by layer, breath by breath.

Take a few moments to become aware of your body.

Chapter Ten

Awareness of Thoughts

If you have ever said to yourself, my mind is racing and too busy to stop, you are already aware but just don't know that you are aware.

Most of us live in a constant stream of thoughts. The first thing to realize about thoughts is that they are not facts. They are not commands. They are just... thoughts. You're allowed to see them, hear them, even follow them—but you're also allowed not to.

Our culture tells us, "I think, therefore I am." This reduces the concept of a self to the neural activity of the brain, stuck in HACKlandia. By exploring awareness, you realize something far more liberating: you think, and you are aware that you think, therefore you are something else beyond your thoughts.

This doesn't mean thoughts don't matter or that you should ignore them. It means you don't have to be trapped by them. You can experience the roller coaster of thoughts and emotions while sitting in a comfortable seat, watching the ride rather than being thrown around by it.

In the awareness of thoughts, we become free of them. Not free from them—they're still there—but free of the compulsion to believe, follow, or be defined by or to react to every mental event that arises.

With a mindful awareness perspective, we bring awareness to the fact that thoughts arise. Just like breath. Just like the heartbeat. You are not the one producing them—they're just happening. The key shift is in noticing that they are happening in awareness. You are the awareness that is seeing the thoughts.

The brain is an incredible tool. It's created buildings, spaceships, medical miracles. It stores everything you've learned, every experience you've had, every skill you've developed. This neural activity gives you your personality, your creativity, your ability to solve problems and navigate the world.

But here's what happens: the same brain that can cure diseases and compose symphonies can also generate distressed thoughts, obsessive loops, and stories that keep you trapped in old patterns, false assumptions, reactive habits and stale knowledge. Both capacities exist in the same remarkable organ.

The invitation isn't to get rid of thoughts—that's impossible and unnecessary. What does your brain do? Your brain thinks. And it's okay to have thoughts. Actually, it's really good to have thoughts. The practice is to explore awareness of thoughts and trust that this process is somehow healing.

Many people think meditation is about emptying the mind, creating some kind of thought-free zone where you finally get a break from the mental chatter. If you make it happen this way, it won't last. This idea that you can stop thinking is a beautiful fantasy, but it's not what actually happens—and trying to make it happen usually creates more problems. If you try to get rid of your thoughts, that becomes another thought, another task, another mental project. The effort to not think is still thinking. Another hack.

So what's the alternative?

The idea is to let whatever is happening in the present moment happen. If thoughts arise, you become aware of them. Not stop them, not analyze them, not judge them as good or bad. Just to notice: "Thinking is happening."

When you become aware of your thoughts, something shifts. The thoughts don't necessarily disappear, but your relationship to them changes. They kind of dissolve into the background. There's a shift from being the thought to being the awareness of the thought. Awareness is like a vast open space, and in that space, thoughts can come and go and dissipate into awareness without overwhelming you.

Everyone gets lost in thoughts, pulled away into a fantasy, a past event or a future scenario. You don't even know you are doing it until you become aware—aware of thoughts. Not a failure and not a problem, but a great opportunity to really realize awareness and the awareness of awareness. When you know you are lost in thoughts, you are now aware and now you know it.

Tara Brach, a wonderful mindfulness teacher, developed a framework for mindfulness of emotions that also works with thoughts, so I will introduce it here. It uses the acronym RAIN as a way to know what is going on in your brain and then watching the shift.

(R)ecognize what is happening. Put a name on what's happening. "I'm thinking." "I'm planning." "I'm worrying." "I was lost in thought." "I'm having a brainstorm." "I'm reliving a past event." Now, what is your hack when this happens? Maybe you push everything else aside, or you start judging yourself, or your inner critic takes over the mind's activity. Recognizing what is going on in your brain is the first and perhaps the most difficult step.

(A)llow it to happen. Allow these thoughts and emotions to be present. You are safe, you are in the present moment, allowing them to be there—as difficult as that might be. Remember, you are the awareness of these memories, not the memories themselves. Use your MAP to allow them to be there as part of the present moment—just like the breath and the body.

(I)nvestigate what else is going on. What do you feel in your body and where is this feeling located? What does it feel like? Is it true? Can you be sure? What other thoughts and emotions are rising up along with this. From a mindful awareness perspective, take on the role of detective—see what hacks you are using—what was the assumption you made, what were you taught to be true, what is your habit of reacting? Be aware of how this all fits together, how they all integrate, all the parts of this mental activity.

(N)urture yourself with the compassion that is your essence. Give yourself a break and treat yourself like you would treat your best friend coming to you with this scenario. And as you do this, the whole experience will rise and fall just like the breath while you remain still and calm, with a mindful awareness perspective, and feel the joy that comes from letting all of this be transformed into present moment awareness and the essences that emerge. When we rest in this perspective—when we shift from believing every thought to observing the thought—we begin to see through the illusion that our thoughts define us. They don't. They arise. They pass. And something deeper remains. That's what we're pointing to when we talk about awareness. It's not a thing you can grasp with your thinking mind. It's the space in which all thoughts appear and disappear.

As this practice deepens, the thoughts and stories you once believed were so important begin to naturally fall away. Not because you're rejecting them, not because you let go, but because they simply lose their grip. Things that used to upset you stop being so significant. Old patterns of worry or self-criticism start to feel foreign, like clothes that no longer fit. This isn't something you make happen. It's something you allow to happen by consistently returning to the awareness that's always been here, always been you. Can you see now that what people say is letting go is actually a falling off? You can't let go. Trying to let go is just another problem. When things start to fall off, you may think you let go, but that would be another thought to be aware of. You are not letting go, you are letting be.

Chapter Eleven

Awareness of Emotions

If thoughts are like clouds in the sky, emotions are like weather systems. Sometimes sunny, sometimes stormy, and often unpredictable. But just like weather, they are natural—and they move. Emotions are not the enemy. In fact, emotions are vital indicators of what matters to us. When we don't bring awareness to them, we either suppress them or get swept away by them. Unrealized emotions turn into moods. You get grumpy, or sad, or anxious—moody. You express it in your body, your posture, your speech. They can last a long time, and you don't really know why. Maybe you feel trapped in this sticky place of yucky emotions with no way out—but there is a way.

In the MAP approach, there is a shift from denying and burying or being overwhelmed by moods and emotions to instead letting them be in the space of awareness. You then feel emotions fully, without believing, judging or let them overwhelm you. But emotions are tricky and percolate at a deep level, making us feel moody and uncomfortable without knowing why. On the 4+2 Path, we stop to take a closer look.

The first and most important thing to do is recognize that an emotion or mood is there, stirring.

The RAIN instructions for thoughts apply to emotions. The (R)ecognition phase allows us to see our moods and emotions stirring before being caught by them. It can start just by noticing that you are happy and blissed out, or grumpy, or anxious, or nervous or angry or sad. You don't really know why, but you are. This funk or elation can go on for days and is a loop that just keeps going. We like the good ones and want them to stay—falling in love or getting a new job—it's great! But the bad ones, we don't like, we suppress and do not face. The deeper layers of emotion that result from trauma, breakups, job loss, grief—we don't want to face, and we put them out of our mind for good reason. Recognizing them and then (A)llowing them would be cruel if we did not have a MAP to transform them into presence. Allowing opens up the possibility of being present to see the past as the past and the future as the future. With the MAP, we can allow the emotion to be present, just like being aware of the breath. Allowing the emotions opens up the space for (I)nvestigation of the main emotion or mood and the other associated ones feeding or following along. For example, with anger, what other emotions are contributing to the expression? Was there an insult, an unmet expectation, and did that trigger an emotion of helplessness and "this always happens"? Many of us learned these reactions as children and have never stopped that loop. It's another one of those hacks. Investigation is like being your own therapist, and if that's too hard on your own, talk to one—they can help with this allowing and investigation. You can also become aware of how emotions show up in the body. Fear might tighten your chest. Sadness might settle in your throat. Anger might burn in your belly or face. Again, it's all about bringing the MAP to this investigation, so that you can rest as awareness. We bring mindful awareness to the sensations of the emotion—not the story it tells, not the justification for it. Just the raw feeling. We let it be felt. This can be hard. Emotions can be intense. But they are temporary, especially when you allow them to move through. The only way out is through.

Now that this mood or emotion is out there fully seen and investigated, you hold it in awareness. Then what do we do with them? Remember the essences—the joy of being, peace and equanimity, unconditional love and compassion that we all have at our core, discovered through our return to our true nature? Use these to (N)urture yourself, see the hacks that led to this and be compassionate with yourself and all that you have been through, all of the complicated scenarios that arose. Here in the present moment, you are safe, solid and are more than these things coming and going in your brain. The past is gone, and the future is yet to come. Being present in loving awareness is all that there is—find the solace and joy that comes from this realization. Rest as awareness, you have returned, you are home.

Awareness is the space that can hold even the strongest emotion. So, we sit with emotion like we would with a crying child. We don't try to fix it. We don't walk away. We hold it gently. In time, the emotion changes. It reveals something. Often, underneath anger is hurt. Underneath hurt is care. Underneath it all is love. And that's the beauty of this practice: with mindful awareness, emotions are not obstacles—they're gateways. They open us up to our deeper humanity. They connect us to others. They make us real. And once you realize you can sit with even the strongest emotion, something in you relaxes. You're no longer afraid of feeling. And that is profound freedom.

Chapter Twelve

Awareness of Awareness

Let's talk about one of the most subtle but powerful aspects of the Mindful Awareness Perspective: awareness of awareness itself. Now that we've explored breath, body, thoughts, and emotions, this is the place where all of it begins to merge. This is the moment when mindfulness becomes something greater than technique—it becomes presence itself. This is how mindfulness works. Awareness of awareness is the heart of the Mindful Awareness Perspective. It may sound abstract at first, but it's incredibly grounded and real. This is not a trick of the mind or a philosophical curiosity—it's something experiential and available to you now.

When you become aware of your breath, or your body, or your thoughts or emotions, you're tuning into a level of presence that's often bypassed. It may seem like mental awareness at first. But there's another layer to this—a layer that notices not just the breath or the thought, but the act of noticing itself. That's what we mean by awareness of awareness. It's that moment where you suddenly realize, "I'm aware that I'm aware." Not in a mental way, not as an idea, but as an experience. There's a shift from getting caught in the contents of your mind to becoming the space in which all of that arises. You start to see that awareness is not something you do—it's something you are.

This shift opens a new dimension of being. You're no longer just the thinker or the feeler—you're the field in which thinking and feeling happens. Awareness of awareness doesn't mean you disappear or become detached. On the contrary, it brings you into life more fully. From this stance, you can embrace your experience—messy or beautiful—as it is, without judgment.

It also reveals the essential qualities that are so often overlooked. In this space, you find not only stillness, but a peace that has no opposite. A joy that doesn't depend on anything. An unconditional love that arises spontaneously. Compassion not based on effort or obligation, but born naturally from recognizing your shared being with everyone else.

This isn't a technique to master. It's a recognition of something that's always been there. And like everything in the map to the MAP, it's not something you force—it's something you allow. When the mind relaxes in the present moment, when you stop chasing the next moment or resisting the current one, this deeper awareness shines through.

And here's the beautiful part: this awareness is the same in all of us. It's not personal. It doesn't have a name or a history. When you rest in awareness of awareness, you rest in what's common to all beings. You begin to recognize yourself in others—not conceptually, but viscerally. It's what makes love natural. It's what makes generosity effortless. It's what makes wisdom intuitive.

This is why awareness of awareness is not just another layer—it's the transformative one. It's the place from which all true change, insight, and healing emerge. It's the overlooked treasure that turns out to be the source.

And it's always right here for the noticing.

We've learned how to adopt a stance—a way of being—that allows us to witness our experience instead of just being swept away by it. It's not a perspective you have to create; it's one you already have but likely haven't lived from. And when you start to use it, something fascinating happens: what was unconscious starts to become conscious. Thoughts, emotions, habits—they begin to surface. And yes, some of what surfaces might be uncomfortable. But this is where transformation begins.

While we laid out the four foundations in a linear order, the truth is that real awareness is not linear. Breath, body, thoughts, and emotions—these aren't separate streams. They're aspects of the same river. And awareness flows through them all. Awareness of awareness is like stepping back from the riverbank and seeing the whole landscape. You recognize that you are not only the river—you are the one seeing all that is happening in it.

Mental awareness is different from this deeper awareness. Mental awareness observes. Awareness of awareness witnesses the observer and the whole if it is your present moment experience. It's the subtle realization that you're not just watching your breath, or your thoughts, or your feelings—you're watching the one who watches. And something incredible happens here: presence emerges. Without judgment. Without resistance. Without needing to change anything. It's a space of quiet knowing, and in that space, you feel something many people have searched for their whole lives: peace.

Not the peace that comes from everything going your way, but the peace that comes from knowing you don't need everything to go your way. You're okay. This moment is okay. Even if it's hard. From that peace emerges joy. Not the excited joy of reward or success, but a calm joy. A joy that has no opposite. It's just the joy of being. You're here. You exist. And it's enough.

And from that joy, love arises. A natural love. Unforced. Friendly. Kind. You stop judging yourself so harshly. You stop needing everyone else to be different. You start feeling the connection that's been there all along. Your love will not be based on conditions, met expectations, false assumptions, or even fixed knowledge. Your love will be unconditional—even if your brain says no way. Being aware of the way you react transforms the reaction into presence and allows a response.

This is what we mean when we talk about the unity of all beings. This is why, when we rest in awareness of awareness, we begin to understand the deeper truths that religions point toward—truths about compassion, unity, forgiveness, grace. Not because we believe them, but because we know them, from the inside out. This doesn't mean you abandon your life. It means you start living it differently. With more alignment. With more compassion. With more clarity. With new knowledge gained from the Mindful Awareness Perspective.

So, let's say it clearly: awareness of awareness is not the final destination—it is the return. You can return with one breath. One moment of seeing. One act of allowing awareness.

And once you step through, you begin to understand you're already home.

Chapter Thirteen

The Unity of All Beings

One of the most profound realizations that emerges from working with the Mindful Awareness Perspective is this: at our core, we are not separate. We are expressions of the same fundamental awareness, differentiated only by the conditioning, the hacks, we've picked up along the way. The unity of all beings isn't a philosophy or an abstract idea—it's something we can directly experience when we rest deeply in awareness.

This unity is not something we create. It's something we remember. It's revealed as we peel back the layers of habits, assumptions, and conditioning that form the illusion of separateness. When awareness rests in itself—when we're not caught up in the noise of thoughts and emotions, of fear and regret—we glimpse something so simple, so obvious, that we often overlook it: we are not alone. We are not divided. We are not other.

This realization isn't about dissolving our uniqueness or pretending we're all the same. It's about recognizing that our differences emerge from a shared ground—a universal field of awareness. Within this awareness, there's space for everything: every story, every struggle, every identity. But they're all held in something larger, something shared. The boundaries between us soften. And in that softening, we find peace.

I've seen this unity most clearly in the delivery room, witnessing the first breath of a new human being. In that moment, what's arriving is more than a body—it's pure potential, untouched by the world's conditioning. That first breath is a bridge between formlessness and form, between the unknown and this world of complexity. And every one of us began that way. Every single person you see, no matter how complicated their life appears now, was once that same light, that same miracle of breath and being.

This experience of unity shifts how we live. From a limited, hacked perspective, we protect ourselves, defend our positions, compete for attention or resources. But from awareness, those concerns dissolve. We see the other as ourselves. And that recognition naturally gives rise to compassion—not as a moral obligation, but as a spontaneous movement of love.

This is what the 4+2 Path leads us to. We begin with the breath, move through the body, then thoughts and emotions—not as isolated practices, but as a way to reveal the constant presence of awareness itself. And when awareness becomes aware of itself, something even more extraordinary happens: we realize that awareness isn't confined to one body, one mind. It's the same field shared by all beings.

You don't have to force this realization. You don't have to believe in it. You simply can be aware and notice it. It's already here. Always has been. The path doesn't lead to somewhere new—it leads to that layer where you see clearly what's always been true: that what seemed separate is part of the same whole.

And this is not just for you. This realization is the beginning of a new way of living in the world. When you act from this awareness, you bring something into the world that it desperately needs: authenticity, peace, generosity, connection. You become a source of love not because you try to be, but because love is the natural movement of awareness when it recognizes itself in all beings.

We live in a time where separateness is often amplified, even celebrated. But you don't have to play that game. You can return to the source. You can live from the place where nothing is missing, nothing is broken, and everything belongs. And from that place, you can help others return home too.

The unity of all beings is not a dream—it's the most real thing there is. You've already touched it. Maybe just for a second. Maybe without realizing it. But it's there, and it's waiting for you to remember.

Let this be your invitation to keep going. To keep uncovering. To live not from fear or separation, but from the steady, generous, joyful awareness that knows: we are one.

Chapter Fourteen

Discovering and Living from a New Kind of Knowing

In our path from HACKlandia to MAPtopia, we began by examining something central to our lives but rarely questioned: how do we know what we know? How do we acquire knowledge? This is a journey not only of awareness but also of understanding the nature and source of knowledge itself. The shift from HACKlandia to MAPtopia isn't merely geographical—it's epistemological, a change in how we know and what we consider true.

HACKlandia is the land of habits, assumptions, conditioning, and the kind of knowledge that is passed down, taught, memorized, or absorbed without much examination. It is the world shaped by our past experiences, our upbringing, our culture, our biology. It is the realm of the mind as a product of history—personal, familial, social, even evolutionary.

As a physician, I know this realm well. Medical school, and much of life in the sciences, is about acquiring knowledge—factual knowledge, technical knowledge, procedural knowledge. We study, memorize, analyze, and apply. This kind of knowledge has given us antibiotics, surgery, heart transplants, and neuroscience. It is essential, and I would never diminish its value. But it is not the only kind of knowledge available.

What I didn't realize until much later—until I began really exploring awareness—is that there's another kind of knowing. A different source. It can't be memorized. It's not found in textbooks. No one can hand it to you. This is the inner knowledge that only reveals itself when we become quiet enough to listen. It's the knowing that arises not from thought, but from awareness.

Let's take a wider view for a moment. Expand the aperture of your attention. Your genes hold vast knowledge. Your body knows how to live. Your heart knows how to beat. Your lungs breathe. Your cells metabolize and replicate. The innate biological knowledge of your body is staggering, and most of it unfolds without conscious participation. Even scientists, brilliant as they are, have only scratched the surface of this embodied intelligence.

But here's the leap: just as your body holds knowledge for survival, your deeper awareness holds knowledge for being. It holds the blueprint—not for how to fix or control the world—but for how to live in alignment with truth, love, joy, peace, and freedom. This inner knowledge is not a theory. It is a direct experience.

To access it, get out your compass, use the map to the MAP, shift to a mindful awareness perspective. Enter the present moment—not as a concept, but as a lived space where past and future fall away.

In that space, you are no longer evaluating, comparing, judging, or strategizing. You are simply aware. And in that awareness, knowledge emerges—not as a thought, but as a knowing.

It might begin subtly. A felt sense of peace. A quiet joy that has no opposite. A wave of unconditional love, not for anything in particular, but simply because love is the texture of this awareness. You might feel clarity. Intuition. Compassion—not as an emotion but as a presence. And in these qualities, you begin to know something deeper than you've ever known before.

This is the knowledge of MAPtopia. It is the knowledge that emerges when we cross the threshold to awareness of awareness. And this knowledge changes everything.

In HACKlandia, our culture/society/education system taught us to know in order to fit in, control, compete, and succeed. We absorbed cultural truths that often aligned with tribalism, separation, fear, and scarcity. These truths shaped our identities, our goals, our relationships. And yet, something within us always whispered that something was missing. That there was more. That we were out of alignment with our deeper selves.

That whisper is the pull of the compass, the call to MAPtopia. It's the yearning of your true nature asking to be remembered.

When we arrive in MAPtopia—when we've used the map to the MAP and the 4+2 Path to explore our inner landscape—we find that knowledge is not a goal. It is a revelation. It is what happens when we stop looking outside and start resting as awareness. And the knowledge we receive there is not just about ourselves. It is knowledge that illuminates our interconnection with all beings.

This is the unity we discover through awareness of awareness. It's not an abstract unity. It is not a spiritual platitude. It's a lived experience. And from that experience, our behaviors begin to shift. We don't need to be told to be kind—we simply are. We don't need rules to regulate generosity—it arises naturally. We don't need fear to keep us in check—because we are already connected, already whole.

Now, here's the final step in the journey: we bring that knowledge back to HACKlandia. We don't reject the hacks. We don't leave HACKlandia behind. We re-enter it with new eyes. With new knowledge. The knowledge we acquired in MAPtopia is not meant to sit on a mountaintop. It's meant to be lived. Shared. Embodied. We return to our habits and conditioning not to be controlled by them, but to transform them with awareness. We become agents of a new kind of knowledge in a world still dominated by the old. And we do it not with anger or resistance, but with compassion and clarity.

This, then, is the full arc of transformation. From HACKlandia to MAPtopia and back. From conditioned knowledge to awakened knowledge. From separation to unity. From survival to presence. From belief to direct knowing. The MAP doesn't just get you out—it brings you home. It helps you see that the treasure you were looking for isn't at the end of the path. It's been with you the whole time. You just needed to shift, become present, and become aware.

And now that you are, everything changes.

Chapter Fifteen

Beyond This Way and That Way Is a Third Way

What in the past seemed like the only way... isn't. Even when it feels like there are only two choices—fight or flee, push or give up, fix or avoid—there's still another way. And even if that doesn't make sense to the mind, the moment you notice that you're aware of even thinking that... a new space opens up. That's the third way.

A mindful awareness perspective is not another strategy to replace the ones that aren't working. It's not a technique or a task. It's a shift in perspective—a movement from within that changes how everything is seen. The third way is what naturally emerges when you begin to live from that perspective. It's not an alternative method; it's a different dimension of being.

From the MAP, the choice isn't just between doing more or giving up. It's about recognizing that you are not trapped in the binary at all. You're not stuck between "this way" and "that way." You're the one who can see both. And in that seeing, something deeper becomes available. Not a clever workaround or a spiritual trick, but a real, grounded experience of presence.

The third way isn't about becoming someone else. It's about realizing the awareness that's already here. And if you try it and it doesn't land? That's fine. You haven't broken anything. You can always return to your old ways of coping and figuring things out. But maybe you'll pause and ask: what is it I've really been looking for?

What if what you've been seeking is the very awareness that's been watching the seeking all along? What if the peace you want doesn't come from choosing the right path but from seeing the whole landscape differently?

The MAP reveals this. It helps you recognize the simple presence that's been overlooked, not because it's hidden, but because it's too close. When you begin to live from mindful awareness, the need to figure it all out relaxes. You begin to trust what you see from that perspective—because what you see from there isn't distorted by fear, habit, or identity.

Most of what fills our minds—thoughts, reactions, judgments, defenses—are patterns. They once had a purpose. They helped us survive. But now, they often just spin. The MAP doesn't fight those patterns; it simply shines a light on them. It allows you to see clearly, without identifying with the noise. And from that clarity, the third way begins to show itself.

This modern life—with its complexity, its busyness, its relentless demands—oddly gives us the conditions to make this shift. Because when so much doesn't work anymore, we're left with a rare opportunity to ask deeper questions. And in that questioning, presence appears.

Not just survival.

Not just habit.

Not just reactivity.

But mindful awareness of awareness.

The third way.

This is what the Mindful Awareness Perspective offers. Not just a tool to manage stress or find calm, but a way of seeing that reveals another way of being. One that doesn't depend on external circumstances. One that isn't based on getting things right or solving every problem. It's not a neutral middle point—it's an entirely different vantage point. From the MAP, things that once seemed urgent lose their grip, and things that truly matter become clearer.

Once you glimpse this, even briefly, you'll know what I mean. And from there, you're not following someone else's path—you're walking your own, informed by something deeper than thought, and more trustworthy than fear.

The third way isn't far. It's not special. It's not hidden.

It's here.

It always has been.

Chapter Sixteen

Beyond Detachment— The MAP of Authentic Engagement

A common misunderstanding about awareness practices—especially awareness of awareness—is that they lead to emotional detachment or a kind of dispassionate withdrawal from life. This misconception can make the Mindful Awareness Perspective seem cold, empty, or disconnected from the richness of human experience. In reality, the MAP offers something far more profound: a shift from detachment to authentic engagement.

Detachment often looks like a protective withdrawal. It involves cutting off from feelings, relationships, and circumstances in an effort to avoid being overwhelmed. It's a numbing strategy—an inner stance that says, "I won't let this affect me." It can feel safe, even mature, but in doing so, this attitude blocks access to joy, love, vitality, and connection. It makes us a spectator of life, rather than a participant.

This form of detachment is a reaction—a learned habit from HACKlandia. It's what happens when awareness is still filtered through the lens of fear and defense. And while it may feel like peace, it's actually a kind of absence. The MAP doesn't invite that. The invitation is not to disconnect from life, but to show up with clarity, openness, and responsiveness.

Emptiness is another word out there that goes along with disconnection and is misunderstood. The emptiness we're talking about here is just another word for the potential for spaciousness. It's like nothing is sticking, and everything is possible. This is a key clarification. What the conditioned mind calls "empty" is often just what it feels like when it isn't being constantly filled. Without distraction, stimulation, or habitual identity, it may first register as void. But awareness is never actually empty. It's alive, spacious, and awake.

And here's the important shift: if emptiness arises, that too can be held in awareness. If there's awareness of emptiness, then the emptiness is no longer consuming—it's being seen. And being seen is the beginning of transformation. When that happens, even the sense of void becomes infused with presence. What was once mistaken for deadness reveals itself as depth. The MAP allows for this shift. It doesn't push away the sensation of emptiness; it welcomes it, rests with it, and allows it to unfold. In that unfolding, the essences—peace, love, joy, wisdom—begin to arise naturally.

There is also a subtle but powerful difference between detachment and objective engagement. Detachment is about withdrawing to stay safe. Objective engagement is about opening up from a place of grounded clarity. With the MAP, rather than building emotional walls, a person learns to create space. And not just any space—this is spacious awareness. It's not hollow, but full of potential. From this perspective, emotions, relationships, and challenges can all be fully felt without taking over. The person remains present, steady, and real. The difference lies in the source of response. Detachment comes from fear. Objective engagement arises from presence. One is a habit of mind. The other is a way of being.

Dispassion can also be confused with indifference. Dispassion doesn't mean not caring. It means caring wisely. It means being able to see clearly and act appropriately without being entangled in reactivity. Dispassion allows us to act fully, with purpose and engagement, but without getting hijacked by ego or outcome. It's not turning away. That's something else—something closer to disregarding, which is a kind of refusal to witness. The MAP doesn't invite that kind of bypass. It invites seeing and then responding from something deeper.

Chapter Seventeen

Living from MAPtopia

At this point in the exploring awareness journey, we pulled out our compass (our intention), we've moved to the edge of HACKlandia and started along the 4+2 Path, discovered the MAP, and touched the realization of MAPtopia. We have seen the hacks, and now we know how to MAP them.

We see how the 4+2 Path opens doorways into breath, body, thoughts, emotions, awareness of awareness, and finally, the unity of all beings. The journey has been inward, experiential, and eye-opening.

But now comes the real question: how do you live from this?

How do you bring this perspective into everyday life? Not as a practice done in retreat or on a cushion, but as a living, breathing orientation throughout the day. Let me be clear: this is not about doing more. It's about being different in the doing and the being. It's about returning to the MAP as often as possible—not with effort or striving, but with willingness. Willingness to pause, to pivot, to notice. We do this by weaving awareness into ordinary moments. A few minutes of daily practice can ground the MAP as a stable thread running through your day. But it doesn't require a formal meditation space. Life itself is your practice space.

Here's the key: the realization of the essences, and of the unity of all beings, transforms everything. This is what dissolves HACKlandia. Not by tearing it down, but by seeing through it. When you live from awareness, things don't necessarily look different on the surface. You still go to work, answer emails, care for others, face challenges. But something underneath has shifted. The motivation. The stance. The knowing.

What begins to emerge when we rest in the MAP is a natural movement—a kind of guidance that doesn't need to be figured out. Actions don't arise from scripts or strategies. They come from essence.

When you occupy the MAP, *YOU* are awareness itself. And decisions, movements, and responses start to emerge from the essences that were always there beneath the noise—peace, love, joy, generosity, wisdom, intuition. You don't force them; you remember them.

Instead of reacting out of habit or trying to meet others' expectations, we begin to move authentically. From that authenticity, engagement is not only possible—it becomes inevitable. We see what needs to be done and do it. We see where connection wants to happen and allow it. This kind of living doesn't come from detachment. It comes from full presence.

There is a beautiful paradox at the heart of the MAP: the more we rest in awareness, the more freely and fully we can engage with life. Without the need to protect a false identity or control every outcome, there is space to be real. And in that space, everything becomes more immediate, clearer, and more intimate. This is not freedom from life. This is freedom within life. The ability to remain centered while fully present to whatever arises. The ability to move, speak, create, love, and respond from a place that isn't grasping or resisting.

What falls away is not emotion or ambition—it's entanglement. What's left is engagement rooted in clarity. Presence that doesn't fade. And a kind of fullness that doesn't come from what's added, but from what's uncovered.

There is no need to fall into a void of emptiness. When awareness is here, even emptiness becomes spacious. Even silence becomes alive. Even stillness begins to move. This is not detachment. This is freedom. You begin to live from love, not fear. From peace, not pressure. From presence, not programming. The boundaries that used to divide you from others begin to blur. You recognize your shared essence in the checkout clerk, the angry driver, the crying child, the lonely elder. This isn't a belief—it's a felt reality. And from there, you don't need to try to be kind. You are kindness. You don't try to forgive. Forgiveness flows naturally. You don't try to be mindful. You are awareness itself. This is not some ideal to reach. It's what you've always been. Now you just know it because you are shining light on your deeper knowingness.

So start here. Today. With one breath. With one pause. With one moment of noticing.

And let that moment open the door to all the others.

Welcome home!

Chapter Eighteen

Simple Daily Practices

Daily Triggers for MAP Moments

You don't have to wait for the perfect time to reconnect with the MAP. Here are some simple, natural triggers for MAP moments throughout the day:

Getting ready for the day. Taking a shower, or brushing your teeth, think to yourself "I'm brushing my teeth" and ask, How do I know that? Who am I? The MAP will tell you.

Getting into the car. Put something in your car to remind you to MAP the return to yourself. Use your breath, body and thoughts about your "to-do" list and transform them into presence.

Red lights. When you stop at a traffic light, stop in your mind too. Take one breath. Notice the present moment.

Washing your hands. Use this as a moment to pause. Feel the water, the temperature, the motion. Be present.

Feeling overwhelmed or stressed. Instead of spiraling, pivot. Name what's happening. Feel your breath. Rest as awareness of all the hacks, the brainstorming. Use your compass and your MAP to point the way forward.

Moments of sadness or disappointment. Place a hand on your heart. Feel the emotion. Let it be known. Let it pass through awareness. Feel the emotion and the Joy of Being at the same time.

Walking into a room. Pause before you enter. Be aware of your body. Set the intention to be present. Feel into how the MAP leads to the Unity of All Beings. They are just like you, despite their hacks.

Seeing another person. Whether it's a patient, a colleague, a stranger—remember, they are part of the same field of awareness. Be with them in healing presence. Compassion is your essence.

Simple Practice

Just 3 to 5 minutes a day, with the intention to rest in the MAP, can have a profound effect. You can find a comfortable spot, put your phone away (or just use it as a timer) sit in a chair, drink your coffee with awareness and use the map to the MAP. You can add minutes as your mind starts to quiet down. When the urge arises to stop, notice that hack and let it pass.

Find a quiet place. Sit, stand, or lie down. No special posture is required.

Feel the breath. Become aware of the breath. No need to change it. Just let it be. Knowing that you are breathing is different from unconscious breathing. You are already connecting to a mindful awareness perspective.

Notice the body. Feel your weight, the contact with the ground or chair, the sensations. Scan from your feet to the top of your head, becoming aware of all of the functions of the organs, even the brain. See the body as it is today. Watch the reaction, respond with wisdom.

Notice thoughts. Are they present? Are they pulling you in? Or are they just moving through? When you know your thoughts are racing, you are awareness. Rest as awareness.

Notice emotions. What is your current emotional state? What is your mood? What's underneath? Can you see this with awareness, and allow it to be just as it is?

Rest as awareness. Drop into the space that is aware of awareness. Not thinking about it—but being aware that you are aware. Again, rest as awareness.

Sense the unity. Everyone's hacks are different, but awareness is universal. In that space, notice what qualities begin to emerge. Love. Peace. Joy. Connection. Let them arise. Let them be. Take them with you throughout the day.

There is no right or wrong here. Just repeat the cycle. Every time you know you have drifted, you are aware. You're already there.

Epilogue: The Path Continues

This is not the end.

The MAP doesn't conclude with the final chapter. It continues each moment you remember to rest as awareness, each time you pivot from habit to presence. The 4+2 Path culminating in the realization of MAPtopia— awareness of awareness and resting as awareness, the understanding of unity—they are not trophies to earn. They are invitations that keep unfolding.

There will be days you forget. There will be moments you lose the thread. That's not failure—that's the rhythm of returning. Every time you find yourself back in HACKlandia, you get another chance to remember. To look again. To align again. To open.

Remember, anytime you think you're not doing it right, anytime you realize you're lost in thoughts, anytime the inner critic yells at you or judgment arises, that's the moment you can pivot. You can transform those old hacks into presence. That is the practice. That is the power.

And now that you have the MAP, others will sense something different about you. Your relationships will deepen. Your choices will be different. You are on a new road, heading to a new destination. And know this: you are not alone. We are all on this same journey.

I'll see you there. And when we meet, we'll give each other a knowing fist bump. And if you need a hug, I've got that too.

Living from MAP is not about transcending life. It's about fully inhabiting it. As you sweep the floor. As you talk to your child. As you get bad news. As you sit in stillness or walk in noise. In all of it, awareness is available. The essences are here. The unity is present.

You are not separate from what you seek.

You are not far from peace or joy or love or compassion.

You are already the field that holds it all.

Let this not be a closing, but a turning.

Toward your own life.

Toward this moment. Again and again.

This is your path now.

Keep walking.

And don't forget to look around—you're not walking it alone.

About the Author

Frank Anderson, MD, MPH, is a board-certified obstetrician-gynecologist and Fellow of the American College of Obstetricians and Gynecologists, public health professional, educator, certified mindfulness teacher, and contemplative practitioner whose career spans clinical medicine, academic leadership, global health, and the study of awareness.

He earned his medical degree and completed residency training in Obstetrics and Gynecology at the University of Tennessee and later completed a Master of Public Health at the Johns Hopkins Bloomberg School of Public Health. While at Johns Hopkins, he served on the faculty in the Department of Obstetrics and Gynecology at the Johns Hopkins Hospital, where his early academic work focused on maternal health and community-based approaches to care.

Dr. Anderson then moved to the Navajo Nation, where he served as Chief of Obstetrics and Gynecology for the Indian Health Service hospital in Chinle, Arizona. This immersive clinical role shaped his lifelong commitment to health equity, cultural humility, and respectful care in underserved communities.

His interest in system-level impact led him to Washington, D.C., where he was selected as a Science & Diplomacy Fellow through the American Association for the Advancement of Science (AAAS).

While at the U.S. Agency for International Development (USAID), he focused on global health policy, with a particular emphasis on maternal mortality reduction strategies.

He subsequently joined the faculty at the University of Michigan, where he combined research, teaching, and global program development to advance maternal health systems. Promoted to full Professor, he studied academic partnerships in sub-Saharan Africa—particularly in Ghana—designed to build sustainable, locally led obstetric and gynecologic capacity. He now holds the title of Professor Emeritus.

In parallel with his clinical, academic and policy work, Dr. Anderson has spent decades engaged in contemplative practice and inquiry. He trained with Thai forest monks, Korean Zen teachers, Soto Zen teachers and contemporary nondual guides. He is a certified mindfulness teacher through the Mindfulness Meditation Teacher Certification Program (MMTCP), led by Jack Kornfield and Tara Brach. He co-founded Open Mindfulness Meditation, an ongoing community-based and online mindfulness group in Ann Arbor that continues to support people in their exploration of awareness and presence.

His personal and professional journey led to the development of the Mindful Awareness Perspective™ (MAP), a contemporary framework for training people to recognize and live from the innate human capacities of equanimity, love, joy, compassion and presence. MAP is not just a technique to master, but a way of seeing that is always available and deeply transformative when realized.

He is the founder of the Mindful Awareness Institute, where he trains physicians, therapists, and professionals to embody and teach the MAP in both personal and professional contexts.

Dr. Anderson is also the co-creator and co-host of the Exploring Awareness podcast, a 63-episode series of real-time, unscripted dialogues on awakening and mindful presence. Co-hosted with journalist

Lisa Barry for the first 62 episodes, the podcast invites listeners to explore awareness not as a concept, but as a lived experience grounded in daily life.

He is currently in private practice in Miami, Florida.

To learn more about his work, listen to the Exploring Awareness podcast, and visit his website or @frankwjoe on Substack and social media.

Appendix I: Where to Go From Here

We have discussed the root—that indescribable part of our human experience that is beyond the hacks, in that layer of awareness behind everything we do. Roots are part of a plant; they look alike, but they are part of different trees, with different branches and flowers. It's just like that in the world of exploring awareness, as people use words and culture and history to express and guide others to the root. Exploring these expressions opens a whole new world of discovery.

In this day and age, we have access to all of it. Expressions from every corner of the world can be studied and practiced any other place in the world. You can find Buddhist temples in Africa, and African temples in the US.

Now that you know the root, here are some favorite teachers and guides who have each shared something essential in pointing toward the Mindful Awareness Perspective.

Our Podcast

Exploring Awareness (Podcast)

A companion to this work—62 episodes of conversations, practices, and guided meditations oriented to mindful awareness and the Mindful Awareness Perspective.

Website:
Podcast: Exploring Awareness — Podcast Feed — https://exploringawareness.org

Poetry and Contemplative Literature

David Whyte

Poet and philosopher who explores the intersection of work, love, and spiritual awakening. David Whyte's poetry cuts straight to the heart of human experience with stunning clarity. His poem "The Well of Grief" can be a lifeline in difficult times. He understands that transformation invites a dive into the dark waters of experience rather than swimming away from them.

Essential Reading: *The Heart Aroused*; *Crossing the Unknown Sea*
Website: https://davidwhyte.com
Podcast: On Being – "The Conversational Nature of Reality" — https://onbeing.org/programs/david-whyte-the-conversational-nature-of-reality/

Contemporary Nondual Teachers

Adyashanti (Stephen Gray)

American spiritual teacher focused on awakening and the end of seeking. Adyashanti (whose name means "primordial peace") has a gift for making the most profound truths accessible without cultural baggage. His approach resonates because he speaks from direct experience rather than borrowed wisdom. As he teaches, don't abdicate your own authority—learn deeply—without giving it away.

Essential Reading: *The Way of Liberation (free PDF); Falling into Grace*

Website: https://www.adyashanti.org

Podcast: Being Unlimited with Adyashanti — https://www.adyashanti.org/podcast

Rupert Spira

Contemporary teacher of the nondual understanding. Rupert Spira's work centers on recognizing our essential nature as pure awareness. Being Aware of Being Aware directly explores what we call the MAP—that shift from identifying with thoughts and experiences to recognizing yourself as the awareness in which they appear.

Essential Reading: *Being Aware of Being Aware; The Nature of Consciousness*

Website: https://rupertspira.com

Podcast: The Rupert Spira Podcast — https://rupertspira.com/podcast

Eckhart Tolle

Spiritual teacher focused on presence and the power of now. Tolle's teaching about presence and awakening from the dream of thought aligns with exploring awareness. The insight that we are "something the universe is doing in the same way the wave is something the ocean is doing" points to interconnectedness.

Essential Reading: *The Power of Now*; *A New Earth*
Website: https://eckharttolle.com
Podcast: Eckhart Tolle: Essential Teachings — https://eckharttolle.com/podcast

Traditional Buddhist Wisdom Made Accessible

Jack Kornfield

Psychologist and Buddhist teacher who bridges Eastern wisdom and Western psychology. Jack Kornfield has been instrumental in bringing mindfulness to the West without losing its transformative power. His evolution from teaching "mindfulness" to "loving awareness" reflects the same journey we take in the MAP—from technique to a way of being.

Essential Reading: *A Path with Heart*; *After the Ecstasy, the Laundry*
Website: https://jackkornfield.com
Podcast: Heart Wisdom (Be Here Now Network) — https://beherenownetwork.com/category/jack-kornfield/

Tara Brach

Psychologist and meditation teacher specializing in radical acceptance. Tara Brach's work on radical acceptance and loving presence offers practical pathways into the heart of awareness. Her RAIN technique (Recognize, Allow, Investigate, Nurture) provides a beautiful framework for meeting difficult emotions with mindful awareness.

Essential Reading: *Radical Acceptance*; *True Refuge*
Website: https://www.tarabrach.com
Podcast: Tara Brach (Talks & Meditations) — https://www.tarabrach.com/talks-audio-video/

Suzuki Roshi (Shunryu Suzuki)

Zen master who brought Soto Zen to America. Zen Mind, Beginner's Mind remains essential. The chapter "Beyond Consciousness" points toward pure awareness—the foundation of the MAP. "In the beginner's mind there are many possibilities; in the expert's, few" captures the open, curious quality of exploring awareness.

Essential Reading: *Zen Mind, Beginner's Mind (see "Beyond Consciousness")*
Website: https://www.sfzc.org
Podcast: San Francisco Zen Center – Audio Archive — https://www.sfzc.org/teachings/audio-archive

Thich Nhat Hanh

Vietnamese Zen master and peace activist. Simple, profound teachings on present-moment awareness. Mindful breathing and walking meditation offer accessible entry points into deeper awareness.

Essential Reading: *The Miracle of Mindfulness*; *Peace Is Every Step*

Website: https://plumvillage.org
Podcast: The Way Out Is In (Plum Village) — https://plumvillage.org/podcasts/the-way-out-is-in/

Bhante Henepola Gunaratana (Bhante G)

Sri Lankan Buddhist monk and meditation master. Mindfulness in Plain English is one of the clearest, most practical meditation guides. It strips away mysticism and cultural overlay to reveal the simple, powerful essence of meditation.

Essential Reading: *Mindfulness in Plain English*; *Beyond Mindfulness in Plain English*
Website: https://bhavanasociety.org
Podcast: Bhavana Society – Audio Resources — https://bhavanasociety.org/resource/audio/

Ajahn Buddhadāsa

Theravada reformer emphasizing the "heart of the Buddha's teaching." Clear, direct insight into Dhamma and the role of natural, unforced awareness.

Essential Reading: *Heartwood of the Bodhi Tree (themes)*; *Suan Mokkh Talks*
Website: https://www.suanmokkh-idh.org
Podcast: Buddhadasa Archives (talks & resources) — https://www.bia.or.th/en/

Mindful Leadership and Practical Application

Marc Lesser

Executive coach and former Zen priest who bridges contemplative practice and leadership. Demonstrates how awareness translates directly into effective, compassionate leadership—the MAP off the cushion.

Essential Reading: *Seven Practices of a Mindful Leader; Finding Clarity*
Website: https://www.marclesser.net
Podcast: Mindful Leadership with Marc Lesser — https://www.marclesser.net/podcast

The Divine Abodes and Essential Qualities

Amanda Gilbert

Meditation teacher specializing in the heart practices (brahmavihārās). Kindness Now shows how loving-kindness, compassion, appreciative joy, and equanimity are not manufactured techniques but natural expressions of an awakened heart when we rest in aware presence.

Essential Reading: *Kindness Now: A 28-Day Guide to Living with Authenticity, Intention, and Compassion*
Website: https://www.amandagilbertmeditation.com
Podcast: Ten Percent Happier – Amanda Gilbert (feature) — https://www.tenpercent.com/podcast

Inquiry and Self-Investigation

Byron Katie

Creator of "The Work" inquiry method. Four questions open a direct path to freedom from suffering thoughts and bring you back to the awareness perspective explored in the MAP.
Essential Reading: *Loving What Is*; *A Mind at Home with Itself*
Website: https://thework.com
Podcast: At Home with Byron Katie — https://thework.com/podcast/

Eva Pierrakos — Pathwork

The Pathwork lectures present a rigorous, compassionate framework for transformation that maps well to the shift from habit to presence.
Essential Reading: *The Complete Pathwork Lectures (online)*
Website: https://pathwork.org
Podcast: Pathwork Lectures (readings/discussions) — https://pathwork.org/lectures/

Ram Dass and the Heart Path

Ram Dass (Richard Alpert)

Spiritual teacher who bridged Eastern wisdom and Western psychology. "The natural state of the mind is pure love, which is not other than pure awareness."
Essential Reading: *Be Here Now*; *Grist for the Mill*
Website: https://www.ramdass.org

Podcast: Ram Dass — Here and Now (Be Here Now Network) — https://beherenownetwork.com/category/ram-dass-here-and-now/

Classic Wisdom

Alan Watts

Philosopher who expressed profound truths in accessible language. "The universe creates people like an apple tree creates apples" points to the organic, natural quality of consciousness.

Essential Reading: *The Way of Zen*; *The Wisdom of Insecurity*
Website: https://alanwatts.org
Podcast: Being in the Way (Alan Watts Organization) — https://beherenownetwork.com/category/being-in-the-way/

Indigenous Wisdom

International Council of Thirteen Indigenous Grandmothers

A reminder that the wisdom of returning to essential nature is ancient and communal. Their message during the pandemic—to see crisis as a portal rather than falling into the hole—captures the transformative potential in every difficult moment.

Website: https://www.grandmotherscouncil.org

Depth Psychology & Symbolic Insight

C. G. Jung

A crucial lens for working with symbols, dreams, and the unconscious—useful for honoring inner images without reducing them to concepts.

Essential Reading: *Modern Man in Search of a Soul*; *The Undiscovered Self*

Podcast: This Jungian Life (independent) — https://thisjungianlife.com

Translators & Texts We've Noted

Thomas Byrom (translator) — The Dhammapada

A lyrical rendering referenced in our discussions.

Essential Reading: *The Dhammapada: The Sayings of the Buddha (Shambhala)*

Start Your Exploration

These teachers are like different paths up the same mountain. Each brings a distinct language, culture, and way of expressing the inexpressible. The root they point to is the same—awareness, presence, and love as your essential nature.

You don't need to study them all. Choose one or two that resonate and go deep. Let their words point you back to your own direct experience. The map to the MAP in this book gives you a foundation for exploring any of these teachings without getting lost in concepts or cultural conditioning. You already know the root. These teachers can help you explore the many branches and flowers that grow from that source.

Start where you are. Use what resonates. Leave the rest. The journey of exploring awareness is yours.

A Final Note and Invitation

I'm currently completing a new book that serves as the deeper foundation for this guide. I've also created the Mindful Awareness Institute to provide training in the Mindful Awareness Perspective™, including certification as a Mindful Awareness Coach. If you'd like to use this program in your own teaching or clinical work, I invite you to join me as part of the faculty cohort. If you're a researcher seeking a clear, replicable approach to test hypotheses about mindful awareness and its outcomes, please join the Institute's research group. All are welcome to participate in our online community and in-person practice and learning conferences.

Appendix II: A Journey of Exploring Awareness

The map to the MAP

In HACKlandia, habits, assumptions, conditioning and (fixed) knowledge—"hacks"—are the main source of knowledge and reactions. An inner source can emerge by exploring awareness, where the Mindful Awareness Perspective (MAP) provides timeless knowledge for a different and authentic life experience.

Use the map to the MAP to guide your journey from HACKlandia to MAPtopia.

Start Your Journey:

• **Awareness of Breath:** Connect to the doorway of awareness—your breath. You've been breathing your whole life but now become aware that you're breathing. This simple awareness of breath is your first step beyond HACKlandia. Set your timer for 3 minutes and just be aware of your breathing...

•**Awareness of Body:** Let awareness spread through your whole body. Notice sensations, comfort, discomfort—they're all welcome in awareness. Your body is always in the present moment. Take 3 minutes to explore awareness of your body...

•**Awareness of Thoughts:** Watch your thoughts arise in awareness. Like clouds in the sky, they come and go. You don't have to follow them or push them away—just be aware of thinking. Spend 3 minutes being aware of your thoughts...

•**Awareness of Emotions:** Let emotions float in awareness. Whether joy or sorrow, recognize, allow, investigate and nurture from present moment awareness. The past is gone, the future is yet to come, Awareness transforms all into pure presence, safe and solid. Rest for 3 minutes in awareness of emotions...

Realizations...

•**Awareness of Awareness:** Who is aware of all this? Rest as awareness itself. This is your home base, always here, always steady. Take 3 minutes to be aware of awareness...

•**Unity of All Beings:** Pure awareness emerges our shared essence—the peace, joy, love and generosity that's everyone's birthright. In awareness, we're all connected. Spend 3 minutes feeling this connection...

Welcome to MAPtopia! From here you can transform HACKlandia through the knowledge gained from your journey. Old patterns naturally dissolve in awareness and the essences of the joy that has no opposite, unconditional love, peace, and compassion arise from within....

Question: How will awareness guide you in sharing this journey with others?

•Remember—the treasure you're looking for, you already have. It's like that story of the beggar sitting on a crate that was full of gold—what you're seeking has been here all along.

•When in doubt, use your compass and this MAP to return home, to return to awareness. You can come back again and again. The peace, joy, love, compassion and generosity are always here, just waiting to be uncovered.

www.ingramcontent.com/pod-product-compliance
Lightning Source LLC
Chambersburg PA
CBHW061802070526
44586CB00023B/2684